NOTES ON PRINTS

NOTES ON PRINTS

by William M. Ivins, Jr.

The M.I.T. Press
Massachusetts Institute of Technology
Cambridge, Massachusetts and London, England

This M.I.T. paperback edition of Notes on Prints
*is an unabridged republication of the first edition
published by the Metropolitan Museum of Art in 1930.*

*The Metropolitan Museum has provided new photographs for
all prints included.*

Library of Congress Catalog Card Number 67-25444

NOTES ON PRINTS

LABELS PREPARED FOR A
SPECIAL EXHIBITION

THE METROPOLITAN MUSEUM OF ART

NOTES ON PRINTS

BEING THE TEXT OF LABELS

PREPARED FOR

A SPECIAL EXHIBITION OF PRINTS

FROM THE MUSEUM COLLECTION

BY

WILLIAM M. IVINS, JR.

CURATOR OF THE DEPARTMENT OF PRINTS

NEW YORK

1930

PREFACE

In 1929 there was made at the Museum an exhibition of
prints and illustrated books selected as though to illus-
trate a short guide to the history of the printed picture.
As an experiment in museum practice the prints were
accompanied by short typewritten labels containing in-
formal conversational comment not only about the
prints exhibited but about prints in general. On the
theory that difference of opinion lends interest to more
things than horse racing, some of these labels were given
a distinctly controversial twist. Of necessity much was
sacrificed to their shortness.

In response to various requests these labels (some of
them in slightly revised form) have been reproduced in
the following pamphlet.

As appreciation of prints requires acquaintance not
only with their pictorial composition but with their actual linear texture, each reproduction smaller than the
original is accompanied by the reproduction of a detail
in the full size of the original.

Saint Onuphrius, German School
5¾ x 4½ *

*These measurements indicate the actual size of each print in inches, height by width.

SAINT ONUPHRIUS

EARLY WOODCUT

GERMAN SCHOOL, LATE XV CENTURY

 The first printed pictures to be made were woodcuts. The earliest of them fall into two groups, playing cards and sacred pictures. These sacred pictures were used much as are their late descendants, our familiar Sunday School cards. Very few if any of them were consciously made as works of art, their function and tradition determining their form. The greater number of them were brightly colored with pigments roughly applied by hand. This print of Saint Onuphrius is late – having been made a generation after men began to make illustrated books – but it is unusually charming in color and is in other respects quite typical of the group to which it belongs.

Page from the block book, Apocalypsis Sancti Johannis, German School
10⅝₁₆ x 7¹¹⁄₁₆

EARLY WOODCUT

PAGE FROM THE BLOCK BOOK
APOCALYPSIS SANCTI JOHANNIS

GERMAN SCHOOL, ABOUT 1460-1470(?)

A page from the second edition of the famous block book of the Apocalypse. The texts as well as the pictures of the block books were cut on wood blocks—from which they get their name. Most of them were gaudily colored by hand. They are generally supposed to have preceded printing with movable types, but all that can be definitely dated are later than the "Gutenberg Bible." It may be that many of them were provincial imitations of type-printed books.

Woodcut from Turrecremata's Meditationes, German School

4 ⅝ x 6 ⅝

EARLY WOODCUT

FROM
TURRECREMATA'S MEDITATIONES
ROME, ULRICH HAN & SIMON NICOLAI CHARDELLA, 1473

GERMAN SCHOOL, 1467

The second edition of the first illustrated book printed in Italy. Its first edition was made in 1467, six years after Pfister at Bamberg made the first type-printed book to contain illustrations. Between 1461 and 1465 Pfister issued eight editions of four illustrated books, of which but fourteen copies are known to survive. This is thus the fifth illustrated book. Although made in Italy it was printed by Germans and its woodcuts were designed by some unknown south German artist. The crudeness of its woodcuts is typical not only of the book illustrations made during the 1460's but of the single-sheet woodcuts of the same period. The history of the woodcut before it began to be used for illustration of printed (and dated) books is largely a matter of learned conjecture.

Woodcut from Boccaccio's De Mulieribus Claris, German School
3 ³⁄₁₆ x 4 ⁷⁄₁₆

EARLY WOODCUT

FROM BOCCACCIO'S
DE MULIERIBUS CLARIS
ULM, ZAINER, 1473

GERMAN SCHOOL, 1473

Just as the Turrecremata of 1467 in the crudeness of its cuts typifies the earliest group of illustrated books, so this Boccaccio, issued by Zainer at Ulm in 1473, may be regarded as one of the best specimens of the second group of German illustrated books. This second group begins shortly after 1470 and is marked by its careful typographic design and the artistic merit of its illustrations. The illustrations in both the first and second groups are by anonymous artists.

Detail of view from Breydenbach's Peregrinationes in Montem Syon, German School
10¾ x 15⁶⁄₁₆

VIEW OF MODON (DETAIL)

BY ERHARD REUWICH FROM BREYDENBACH'S
PEREGRINATIONES IN MONTEM SYON
MAINZ, REUWICH, 1486

GERMAN SCHOOL, 1486

 This book marks the culmination of early German book design. It was the first book to contain either folding plates or specimens of a number of Eastern alphabets. It was also the first illustrated "Baedeker," containing descriptions and advice for travelers to Egypt and the Holy Land.

It is the first type-printed book the pictorial illustrations of which are by a known artist, Erhard Reuwich of Utrecht. Several earlier artists are known by name: Friedrich Walther, painter, and Hans Hurning, joiner, who made a block book at Nordlingen in 1470; Hans Spoerer, who copied earlier block books in 1471 and 1473; Hans Schnitzer of Armsheim, who cut the woodcut maps in the Ulm Ptolemy of 1482; and Taddeo Crivelli and Conrad Sweynheim, who, respectively, engraved the maps in Ptolemies printed at Bologna and Rome in 1477 and 1478; but they do not qualify as illustrators of type-printed books.

Saint John the Baptist in the Desert, by the Master E S
7 $\frac{7}{32}$ diameter

SAINT JOHN THE BAPTIST
IN THE DESERT

ENGRAVING BY THE
MASTER E S

GERMAN SCHOOL, MIDDLE OF THE XV CENTURY

Engraving seems to have been first done sometime early in the fifteenth century. The most important of the second generation of engravers was the Master E S, who was perhaps the first artist to be distinctly conscious of the peculiar qualities of the engraved as distinct from the drawn line. Like most of the other early German engravers he seems to have received his training in a goldsmith's shop. This is shown not only by his elaborate ornamentation, which is conceived in terms of faceted surfaces rather than in terms of flat space relationships, but in his habit of building up his pictures as assemblages of charming details rather than as organized wholes. It is as though his prints were strings of lovely beads of different kinds rather than consistently thought-out necklaces. This is actually a design for a paten.

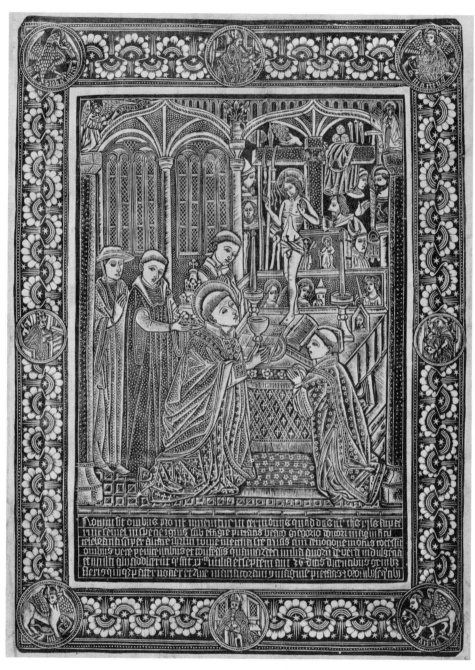

The Mass of Saint Gregory, German School
10 ⅝ x 7 ⁷⁄₁₆

THE MASS OF SAINT GREGORY

EARLY METAL CUT

GERMAN SCHOOL, LATE XV CENTURY

The curious group of *Schrotblätter,* the name given to this kind of engravings, is composed of relief prints from metal plates worked with the silversmith's tools — gravers and punches. In great part the lines in these prints are white on black, and the grounds are filled in with decorative diapers. They bear no relation to the contemporary woodcuts either in conception or in execution. In technique they are most closely related to the early wood engravings of such a nineteenth-century master as Bewick. It is difficult to understand how it happened that their colorful technique was not generally taken up or developed during the Renaissance.

The Virgin in a Courtyard, by Martin Schongauer
$6\frac{9}{16}$ x $4\frac{11}{16}$

THE VIRGIN IN A COURTYARD

ENGRAVING BY

MARTIN SCHONGAUER

GERMAN SCHOOL, BEFORE 1440-1491

Schongauer, in the generation of engravers that came shortly after the Master E S, was the final, most highly developed product of the great early German school. In his work the engraver's technique had lost its tentative, experimental quality, and reached a point where it was perfectly adequate to the demands put upon it. Although for modern classificatory purposes called "a primitive engraver," he came in fact at the end of a more or less definite period, and, so far from being a primitive, shows all the marks that are associated with our phrase *fin de siècle,* such as rather exaggerated elegance, refinement, and lack of vitality, and the knowing, deliberate simplicity that comes from dandiacal self-consciousness. He is thus more akin to Fragonard and Whistler than to Dürer or Rembrandt.

The Lovers, by Israhel van Meckenem

$6 \frac{9}{32} \times 4 \frac{9}{32}$

THE LOVERS

ENGRAVING BY

ISRAHEL VAN MECKENEM

GERMAN SCHOOL, DIED 1503

Israhel, coming between Schongauer and Dürer, and greatly influenced by Dutch art, was one of the first professional engravers in the sense that most of his very many prints were made after the designs of other artists, e.g., those of Holbein the Elder. His original pieces show such a thoroughly bourgeois humor that they may be regarded as the middle-class comic relief to the self-conscious aristocratic elegance of Schongauer. There is reason to believe that he was a practising goldsmith, and his many pattern designs, while lacking the grace and vitality of the ornaments designed by E S and Schongauer, have a certain working practicality not to be found in their work.

Saint Michael Slaying the Dragon, by Albrecht Dürer
15⅛ x 10¹⁵⁄₁₆

SAINT MICHAEL SLAYING
THE DRAGON

WOODCUT BY
ALBRECHT DÜRER

GERMAN SCHOOL, 1471-1528

This illustration from Dürer's Apocalypse, published first in 1498, shows the master as the culminating personality of German Gothic art. Six years later he was to produce his Adam and Eve, in which he solved the major problems of the representation of the nude, and six years after that the Penitent, in which he showed all that he had learned of composition from the Italian painters of the Renaissance. These three prints show his progress from the Gothic ideal to the Renaissance ideal. As he is the only man about whom the several groups of German-speaking peoples have been able to unite in hero worship, it is now almost impossible for anyone to take a justly balanced attitude towards his accomplishment.

Adam and Eve, by Albrecht Dürer

9 ⅞ x 7 ⅝

ADAM AND EVE

ENGRAVING BY
ALBRECHT DURER

GERMAN SCHOOL, 1471-1528

Dürer, by common consent the greatest of German artists, was the first German engraver who was also a painter. This explains more than anything else the solidity of his work and the way in which his prints, as compared with those of his forerunners, are pictures rather than objects of art. He was the only German whose life and work lay in two utterly different climates of thought and opinion. His early work is purely Gothic, his later fully Renaissance. This vast change in attitude is one of the principal reasons for the great fascination he has exercised on later generations. Where the interest of the work of most artists is much less than the sum of the parts of their work, in the case of Dürer it is much greater. For this reason he is one of the very few artists who cannot be adequately represented by a small selection from his work.

The Penitent, by Albrecht Dürer
7 ¾ x 5 ¼

THE PENITENT

WOODCUT BY
ALBRECHT DÜRER

GERMAN SCHOOL, 1471-1528

Of the great artists of his time Dürer was the only one who was at home in many different media. He did epoch-making work in pen, silver point, and chalk drawing, in water-color and oil painting, and in engraving, etching, dry point, and the woodcut. In this sense he was one of the most universal artists of whom we have record. His sturdiness is so great that only after intimate acquaintance with his work is it possible to recognize in it the strong dandiacal element which is one of its most informing characteristics. Without it he would not have been able to excel in so many different media. It is interesting that Ingres should have made a pen and ink copy of this print.

Pilate Washing His Hands, by Lambert Hopfer

5 ⅞ x 3 ½

PILATE WASHING HIS HANDS

ETCHING BY

LAMBERT HOPFER

GERMAN SCHOOL, FLOURISHED 1520-1530

The etching process had long been in use in the armorers' shops as a means of decorating and enriching the smooth shiny surfaces of swords and suits of armor, but it was not until about 1500 that it occurred to anyone to use it as a quicker and easier substitute for engraving in the making of plates from which to strike off printed pictures. Characteristically this quicker and easier substitute was in the beginning used principally for making piratical copies of prints and drawings by better men. It was discovered and developed in this sense by the Hopfer family of Augsburg, one of whom is here to be seen pirating a most celebrated subject from Dürer's engraved Little Passion.

The Emperor Maximilian, by Lucas of Leyden
$10\frac{5}{32}$ x $7\frac{21}{32}$

THE EMPEROR MAXIMILIAN

MIXED ETCHING AND ENGRAVING BY
LUCAS OF LEYDEN

DUTCH SCHOOL, 1494-1533

This portrait, based on one by Dürer, was done in 1520, immediately after the Emperor's death. It is not only the first print in which etching and engraving were used simultaneously, but the first etching that is definitely known to have been made on copper. The earlier etchings were made on iron or steel, materials which after this time were almost never used by engravers or etchers, until in the early nineteenth century hack engravers began to use them again in order to increase the sizes of their editions. This print is therefore a technical monument of the greatest importance. The face is engraved and the architectural background is etched. Lucas also made many very swagger woodcuts.

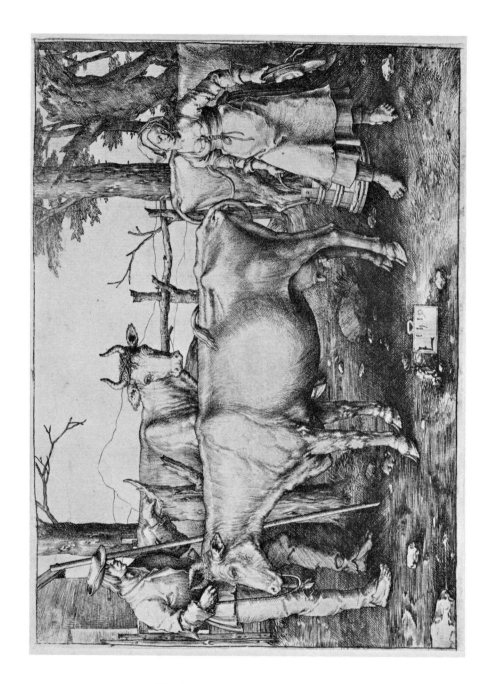

The Milkmaid, by Lucas of Leyden

$4\,^{11}\!/_{16}$ x $6\,^{3}\!/_{16}$

THE MILKMAID

ENGRAVING BY

LUCAS OF LEYDEN

DUTCH SCHOOL, 1494-1533

Lucas had two halves to his head, the one pre-Renaissance Dutch, the other Italianate. In his youthful pure Dutch period he summed up the previous Dutch practice, so that this part of his work may be regarded as the end of a long development. In his later work he came under the influence of Marc Antonio, who had in turn learned much from him. In this period of his work, which is not much savored today, Lucas took the first steps towards that codification of engraving practice which later in the hands of Goltzius became the standardized type of Northern engraving for a long time. The Milkmaid, of Lucas's first period, exemplifies the strong interest in homely genre that is still typical of Dutch artists.

Adam and Eve, by Hans Baldung Grün

$9\,^{13}/_{16}$ x $3\,^{13}/_{16}$

ADAM AND EVE

WOODCUT BY

HANS BALDUNG GRÜN

GERMAN SCHOOL, ABOUT 1476-1545

Of all the German print makers Baldung came nearest to the psychological attitude of Hans Grünewald, striking a note almost unknown in other German prints. In the slang of today, he was an introvert where most of his contemporaries were extraverts. This has greatly interfered with his appreciation by writers and collectors through the centuries, who have regarded him as being "queer" and "uncouth." There seems to be little doubt, however, that despite his comparative lack of fame he is to be regarded as one of the most powerful and certainly one of the most important German artists of his period. None of his fellows had the same tragic, dramatic sense of life.

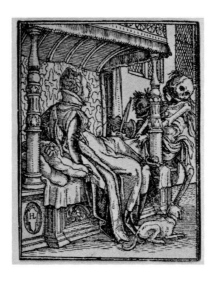

The Duchess and The Ploughman, by Hans Holbein the Younger
2 9/16 x 1 15/16 each

THE DUCHESS   THE PLOUGHMAN

WOODCUTS BY

HANS HOLBEIN THE YOUNGER

GERMAN SCHOOL, 1497-1543

Hans Holbein was a miniaturist and designer of jewels and gold and silver plate. His large paintings were miniatures done big, his woodcuts were miniatures in another medium. Coming from Basle, at the four crossroads of Europe, he was familiar with Italian precedents, and used them constantly to his ends. His woodcuts of the Dance of Death are the final definitive edition of a subject that had occupied Northern thought for more than a hundred years – though the smallest in size, the most powerful of all the versions. More sensitive than Dürer, and with a greater sense of style, Holbein was not so dandiacal as that more powerful draughtsman, with the result that of all the German school he is the most just and the most simple. Alone among his Northern contemporaries he had a feeling for volume and mass. Because of these things he has had a more universal appeal than any other German artist.

(35)

The Judgment of Paris, by Lucas Cranach
14 ⅜ x 10 1/16

THE JUDGMENT OF PARIS

WOODCUT BY

LUCAS CRANACH

GERMAN SCHOOL, 1472-1553

 Cranach, most famous for his dour portraits of Luther and the other reformers, was in reality the most sensuously sensitive of all German artists, having certain interests not wholly dissimilar from those of such a modern Frenchman as Renoir. Now that people are no longer shocked by the thoughts in the backs of their own heads his estimation is undergoing a great change.

The Martyrdom of Saint Sebastian with Two Archers, Italian (Ferrarese) School
8⅜ x 7¾

THE MARTYRDOM OF SAINT SEBASTIAN
WITH TWO ARCHERS

EARLY ENGRAVING

ITALIAN (FERRARESE) SCHOOL, MIDDLE OF THE XV CENTURY

The beginnings of engraving are to be sought in goldsmith's practice. When the goldsmith-engraver began to make pictures he naturally thought in terms of small surfaces richly ornamented with fine detail, rather than in terms of the space, movement, and balance which are associated with architecture and the decoration of large flat surfaces. In Germany the goldsmiths dominated engraving until late in the sixteenth century. In Italy, well before the end of the fifteenth century, engraving came under the domination of painters, sculptors, and architects. Thus engraving had a wholly different development in the two countries, the Germans thinking much of graver-work and its virtuosities, and the Italians paying little attention to it in their absorption in the larger problems of draughtsmanship and pictorial composition. This is one of the earliest prints (1460?-1470) in which no goldsmith's influence is to be seen.

(39)

Arabesque with Attributes of Neptune, Italian School
$2 \frac{13}{16}$ x $1 \frac{11}{16}$

NIELLO — ARABESQUE WITH ATTRIBUTES OF NEPTUNE

EARLY ENGRAVING

ITALIAN SCHOOL, LATE XV CENTURY

This tiny print is typical of the Italian goldsmith's type of engraving. As compared with the German goldsmith-engraver's work it shows a determined pictorial (flat) intention where the other almost invariably seems to be thinking in terms of the chiseled and chased decoration of rounded surfaces.

"Ornament," the technical name for engraved motives and pattern designs for use in the decorative arts, has a history as long and as interesting as that of the printed picture. From the point of view of the student of the history and development of culture it is possibly even more important than the pictorial print, as to a very great extent it was the means whereby knowledge of the different styles passed from one country and generation to another.

The Delphian Sibyl, Italian School

6 31/32 x 4 1/4

THE DELPHIAN SIBYL

EARLY ENGRAVING
IN THE FLORENTINE "FINE MANNER"

ITALIAN SCHOOL, SECOND HALF OF THE XV CENTURY

This Sibyl shows how the early Italian engraver, even though still a goldsmith, kept his work flat and pictorial rather than chiseled and chased as was the German goldsmith-engraver's work. The flat cross-hatching of the Italian is utterly unlike the German chisel work which is always seeking to jump, not into the full round of the sculptor, but into the faceted repoussé and *ciselure* of the maker of gold and silver plate.

Woodcut from Valturius's De Re Militari, Italian School
5¼ x 8½

EARLY WOODCUT

FROM VALTURIUS'S

DE RE MILITARI

VERONA, JOHANNES EX VERONA, 1472

ITALIAN SCHOOL, 1472

The second illustrated book printed in Italy, and the first to contain Italian woodcuts. It is also the first book to contain woodcuts the design of which can be traced to a known artist, as its illustrations are said to have been based upon drawings by Matteo de Pastis, the great medalist. Technically it is very interesting because in one important respect it resembles the first illustrated type-printed book (i.e., the Edelstein, printed at Bamberg in 1461 by Ulric Pfister). The letter press of each of these books was printed first, and, after that had been done, the illustrations were printed in blank spaces left for the purpose, just as we of today fill in blanks in printed forms with rubber stamps. The discovery that types and woodcuts could be printed simultaneously was perhaps the greatest advance made in printing between the time of Gutenberg and the beginning of the last century.

The Battle of Naked Men, by Antonio Pollaiuolo

$15\frac{1}{8}$ x $23\frac{3}{16}$

THE BATTLE OF NAKED MEN

ENGRAVING BY

ANTONIO POLLAIUOLO

ITALIAN SCHOOL, 1432(?)-1498

This Battle of Naked Men is the only print known from the hand of the great Florentine painter and sculptor, Antonio Pollaiuolo. Although it shows a knowledge of the human figure such as no German engraver was to exhibit for at least a generation to come, the whole is kept flat and pictorially decorative as though intended for a large fresco. In the background, however, there are still to be seen strong traces of habits of mind formed in the goldsmith's shop. It is the first print which can pictorially be regarded as a major work of art, its great pattern and the nervous intensity of its draughtsmanship entitling it to a position among the extraordinary manifestations of the Florentine spirit.

The Crucifixion, Italian School
$8\frac{11}{16}$ x $6\frac{7}{16}$

THE CRUCIFIXION

EARLY ENGRAVING
IN THE FLORENTINE "BROAD MANNER"

ITALIAN SCHOOL, LATE XV CENTURY

Long before the Germans, the Italians were producing prints conceived wholly in terms of the pictorial decoration of flat surfaces. In this early Florentine engraving there is to be found little or no trace of that goldsmith's habit of thought which persisted in the work of such a German artist as Dürer until the very end of his life. No one knows who made it but it shows relationships to the work of such famous painters as Lippo Lippi and Alessio Baldovinetti. The advance in technical skill beyond the Ferrarese Saint Sebastian with Two Archers is noteworthy.

The Risen Christ between Saints Andrew and Longinus, by Andrea Mantegna
12½ x 11⅜

THE RISEN CHRIST BETWEEN
SAINTS ANDREW AND LONGINUS

ENGRAVING BY
ANDREA MANTEGNA

ITALIAN SCHOOL, 1431-1506

In this Risen Christ between Saints Andrew and Longinus the three-dimensional flat picture makes its triumphal appearance in engraving. It is one of the epoch-making prints, as it showed that in the hands of a major artist engraving was capable of producing pictures with as great and as serene emotional power and life as any other artistic medium – that engraving was not of necessity restricted to *Kleinkunst*. It is a marvelous example of the way in which true personality breaks through all the bounds of tradition and theory. Its technique is that of Mantegna's pen drawing, severe, restrained, taking no count of textures or color. In hands not as powerful as those of the master this technique became empty and weak.

The Battle of the Sea Gods (left half), by Andrea Mantegna
11 x 16 7/8

THE BATTLE OF THE SEA GODS
(LEFT HALF)

ENGRAVING BY
ANDREA MANTEGNA

ITALIAN SCHOOL, 1431-1506

 With Mantegna the painters came into full dominance over the development of Italian engraving, and Italian prints from his time on became definitely pictorial in intent and conception. Sometimes they were sketches, as in this Battle of the Sea Gods, sometimes thoroughly wrought pictorial conceptions as in the Risen Christ, but no longer is there any trace of the filigreed and minutely faceted metal workers' surfaces of which there is still a vestige in Pollaiuolo's Battle of Naked Men. In no prints prior to these by Mantegna is there to be seen any feeling for volume and mass. The plastic quality of great monumental art makes its first entrance into the printed picture in his work. This print was also one of the great seminal influences in the history of the decoration of flat surfaces.

(53)

The Adoration of the Magi, Italian School after Andrea Mantegna
14 $\frac{1}{32}$ x 10 $\frac{3}{8}$

THE ADORATION OF THE MAGI

ANONYMOUS ENGRAVING AFTER
ANDREA MANTEGNA
ITALIAN SCHOOL, LATE XV CENTURY

In addition to being the first great artist to make a free sketch (The Battle of the Sea Gods) and the first thoroughly wrought-out pictorial composition (The Risen Christ) on the copper, Mantegna was also the first very great artist after whose designs other men made engravings. This Adoration of the Magi is one of the finest examples we have of early reproductive engraving.

Poliphilus before Queen Eleuterylida from Colonna's Hypnerotomachia Poliphili,
Italian School

5 x 5

POLIPHILUS BEFORE QUEEN ELEUTERYLIDA

FROM COLONNA'S
HYPNEROTOMACHIA POLIPHILI
VENICE, ALDUS, 1499

ITALIAN SCHOOL

The "Poliphilus," the only illustrated book printed by Aldus, the most famous Italian printer, has long been celebrated as "the most beautiful of all illustrated books." This is not because its illustrations are the most beautiful pictures to be found in printed books, for they are far indeed from being that, but because among early Italian picture books its illustrations are most completely subjected to, and assimilated in color and line by, the type and the type page. It is as though a book of verse were to be spoken of as the most beautiful of all poetry books because the printed lines of verse made a lovely formal pattern. A learned romance, containing pictures, lists, and descriptions of antiquities and works of art, this book may be regarded as the first, though not the last, imaginative museum catalogue and guide.

Woodcut from Frezzi's Quatriregio, Italian School
3½ x 4⅞

EARLY WOODCUT

FROM FREZZI'S
QUATRIREGIO
FLORENCE, PACINI, 1508

ITALIAN SCHOOL

One of the two most lavishly and beautifully illustrated books produced in Florence by the contemporaries of Botticelli. There were very few Florentine picture books as large as this. Most of them were small chapbooks, and thus, aside from some sermons, they did not get preserved in libraries as did the more learned and bigger books. As compared with Germany Italy had few copperplate engravers during the fifteenth century. Their output was small and, with a few great exceptions, of minor artistic excellence. But woodcut book illustration reached a much higher artistic level in Italy than in Germany.

The Climbers, by Marc Antonio Raimondi
11 3/16 x 8 7/8

THE CLIMBERS

ENGRAVING BY
MARC ANTONIO RAIMONDI
ITALIAN SCHOOL, ABOUT 1480-ABOUT 1530

 Marc Antonio copied the engravings of many Northern artists, notably Dürer and Lucas of Leyden, and in so doing learned many of their tricks and dexterities of graver-work. The trees and foliage of this print are copied from Lucas of Leyden, and the figures from Michelangelo. Marc Antonio combined the German linear scheme for representation of textures and rotundity with the Italian feeling for volumes, and in so doing gave engraving its pictorial enfranchisement.

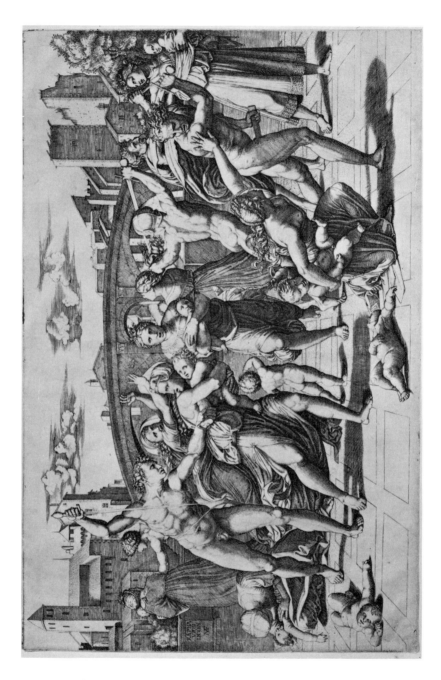

The Massacre of the Innocents, by Marc Antonio Raimondi after Raphael
11⅛ x 16⅞

THE MASSACRE OF THE INNOCENTS

ENGRAVING AFTER RAPHAEL
BY MARC ANTONIO RAIMONDI

ITALIAN SCHOOL, ABOUT 1480-ABOUT 1530

 Starting in Bologna as an amusing but second-rate original engraver, Marc Antonio went to Rome where, working for Raphael, he became the progenitor of the most important line of reproductive engravers the world has ever known. From this time on Italian painters in large measure ceased to make engravings and contented themselves with turning their drawings over to professional engravers for reproduction and publication. Raphael's drawing for this print (in the British Museum) is of the same size, and all along its lines it has been pricked—one of the methods used by the engravers to transfer the outlines of a drawing to a plate.

The Entombment, by Parmigiano
12¹³⁄₁₆ x 9⁵⁄₁₆

THE ENTOMBMENT

ETCHING BY
PARMIGIANO

ITALIAN SCHOOL, 1503-1540

Parmigiano, who died in 1540, and his followers were the first artists to realize that etching was a medium peculiarly adapted to sketching and the quick notation of pictorial ideas—i.e., to the purposes for which it has principally been used in modern times. They came so early in the history of the process that it had not yet been reduced to a general canon of technique. Just as they made their drawings on colored paper and heightened them with white, so did they frequently cover their etchings with blue and green and rose washes and slap in the high lights with lead white. This is to say that they thought of them not as etchings, but as drawings made with the etching process. Because of this they transgress many taboos invented since they were made, and therefore little or no attention has been paid them for almost a hundred years. It is interesting, however, to notice their close spiritual relationship to certain "very modern" things.

(65)

Saint Christopher, by Lucas Cranach
11¼ x 8

SAINT CHRISTOPHER

CHIAROSCURO BY

LUCAS CRANACH

GERMAN SCHOOL, 1472-1553

 The Germans made chiaro-
scuros before the Italians did,
e.g., Cranach's Saint Christopher of 1506, but they were
merely the ordinary German
small detailed black and white
woodcuts complicated by the
addition of color. In Italy the
chiaroscuros, e.g., Ugo da Carpi's Saturn (p. 68), were
thought of as wall decorations, detail was suppressed as
nearly as possible, and emphasis was laid on composi-
tions of large contours and flat spaces differentiated by
slightly varying color. The result was that the Italian
chiaroscuros are the most successful wall decorations
ever made by European print makers.

Saturn, by Ugo da Carpi, after Parmigiano
12 ⅝ x 17

SATURN

CHIAROSCURO

AFTER PARMIGIANO BY UGO DA CARPI

ITALIAN SCHOOL, ABOUT 1450-ABOUT 1525

For the note upon this print see page 67.

One of the twelve sheets composing Pharaoh's Army Submerged in the Red Sea,
by Titian and Domenico dalle Greche
15 ½ x 20 ¾

PHARAOH'S ARMY SUBMERGED
IN THE RED SEA

PART OF THE WOODCUT BY
TITIAN AND DOMENICO DALLE GRECHE

ITALIAN SCHOOL, 1477(?)-1576
FLOURISHED 1543-ABOUT·1558

 Italian and German woodcuts may be contrasted in much the same way as Italian and German engravings. German woodcuts, whether book illustrations or single-sheet cuts, were all made in the same manner, without modification for differences in use. This was the manner of the book illustrators, which grew out of the small, highly detailed miniatures in manuscripts. The large single-sheet German cuts were thus merely small illustrations carried out over larger dimensions. In Italy the large single-sheet cuts were regarded as wall decorations, to be kept flat and with little minor detail – i.e., they are things to be seen at a distance, where the German cuts, no matter how big, have to be seen close at hand. This small portion of Titian's great woodcut is to be contrasted with a similar small portion of about the same size from Dürer's Triumphal Arch.

(71)

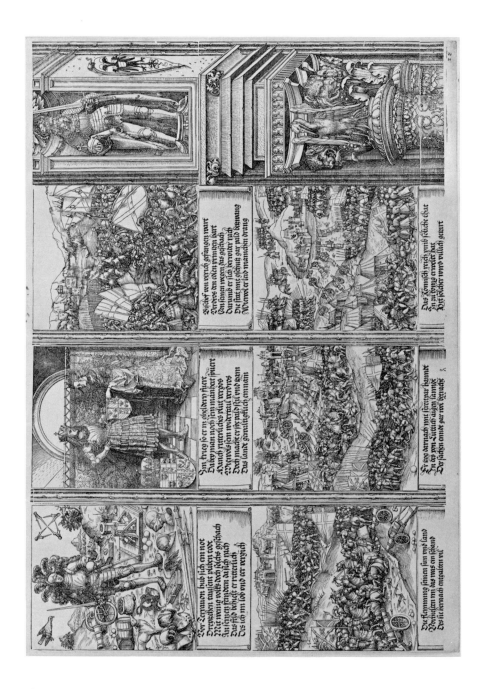

One of the thirty-six sheets composing The Triumphal Arch, by Albrecht Dürer

17 x 24 ⅝

THE TRIUMPHAL ARCH

PART OF THE WOODCUT BY
ALBRECHT DÜRER
GERMAN SCHOOL, 1471-1528

For the note upon this print see page 71 under the heading, Pharaoh's Army Submerged in the Red Sea, part of the woodcut by Titian and Domenico dalle Greche.

Detail of view from Breydenbach's Peregrination, French School
10½ x 15⅝

EARLY ENGRAVING

DETAIL OF VIEW FROM
BREYDENBACH'S PEREGRINATION
LYONS, TOPIE & HEREMBERCK, 1488

FRENCH SCHOOL, 1488

This is the first book with engraved illustrations printed in France, the country in which, subsequently, engraved illustration reached its artistic apogee. These engravings are the first of which we can be sure of the French origin. The earliest experiments with engraved illustration were a Boccaccio printed at Bruges in 1476, the Bolognese Ptolemy of 23 June, 1477 [1462] (the maps engraved by Taddeo Crivelli), and the Florentine Monte Sancto di Dio of 10 September, 1477. The first engravings by celebrated engravers to appear in printed books seem to be the portrait by Cranach on the title of the Wittenberg Heiligthumsbuch of 1509, the illustrations by Jerome Mocetto for the Venetian De Nola of 1514, and the print by Marc Antonio on the title of the Roman Berrutus of 1517. The engravings in this book were copied from the large folding woodcuts in the Mainz edition of 1486.

Page from Heures à Lusaige de Romme, French School

6 7/16 x 4 7/16

EARLY METAL CUTS

PAGE FROM

HEURES A LUSAIGE DE ROMME

PARIS, PIGOUCHET FOR VOSTRE, 1498

FRENCH SCHOOL, 1498

The Paris publishers about 1500 made a great specialty of illustrated prayer books (Horae or Books of Hours), in which are to be found many of the most charming examples of early French graphic art. The printer Pigouchet and the publisher Vostre, who collaborated on this volume, were the most eminent makers of these Horae. In these books there is perhaps to be seen the closest resemblance that early printing affords between the printed book and the illuminated manuscript. The pictures are not woodcuts, but are printed from relief blocks of copper. This book is generally regarded as the highest point in the artistic development of the printed lay prayer book. From a textual point of view it may be regarded as one of the great-aunts of the Book of Common Prayer.

Woodcut from La Bible en Francoiz, French School
8 ¼ x 6 ¾

WOODCUT

FROM

LA BIBLE EN FRANCOIZ

[PARIS, VERARD, AFTER 1500]

FRENCH SCHOOL, ABOUT 1510

Woodcut illustration, like printing itself, did not begin in France until much later than in Germany and Italy. The first book printed in France was issued at Paris in 1470, and the first illustrated book at Lyons on 26 August, 1478. The latter contained woodcuts made in Switzerland. The most important publisher of early French picture books was Antoine Verard of Paris. The illustrations in this undated Bible (about 1510?) are among the finest products of the woodcut school that centered about him. They are typical of the highest development reached by the early French school of printed illustration prior to its breakdown shortly after 1500 under the combined influence of German and Italian precedents and fashions.

Woodcut by Geoffroy Tory from Hore in Laudem Beatissime Virginis Marie,
ad Usum Romanum

$6\frac{5}{16}$ x $3\frac{13}{16}$

WOODCUT BY GEOFFROY TORY

FROM HORE IN LAUDEM BEATISSIME
VIRGINIS MARIE, AD USUM ROMANUM
PARIS, KERVER, 1545

FRENCH SCHOOL, 1525

 After 1500 the influx of German printers into Paris and a muddled general taste brought about a sharp decline in the artistic merit of the prayer books, which lasted until Geoffroy Tory, beginning in the 1520's, issued his epoch-making volumes. Tory was a pedantic professor and editor of texts who, going to Italy, became enthusiastic about the new Italian styles, and, carrying them back to Paris, produced a series of illustrated prayer books which may be regarded as being among the first definitely self-conscious and dandified typographic designs.

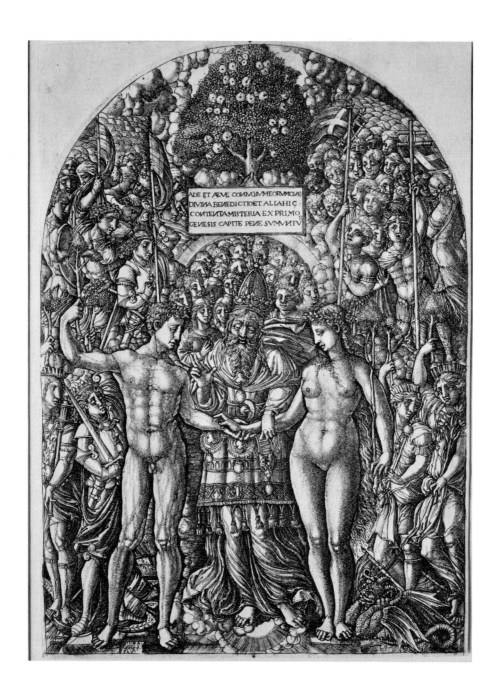

The Marriage of Adam and Eve, by Jean Duvet
11¹³⁄₁₆ x 8⅜

THE MARRIAGE OF ADAM AND EVE

ENGRAVING BY
JEAN DUVET
FRENCH SCHOOL, 1485-ABOUT 1561

Duvet was the first important French engraver, and almost the first in point of time. An unskilled engraver and a derivative artist, getting most of his pictorial ideas from Dürer and Marc Antonio, he found his elected subject in the descriptions of the Apocalypse, of which he made the version that most appeals to the neurotic modern mind. His dependence upon Germany and Italy is typical of most of the engravers of the sixteenth century in France, a country that lagged far behind Germany, Holland, and Italy in its development of the graphic arts.

Summer, after Peter Brueghel the Elder
8¹⁵⁄₁₆ x 11⁵⁄₁₆

SUMMER

ENGRAVING AFTER
PETER BRUEGHEL THE ELDER
DUTCH SCHOOL, ABOUT 1525-1569

Brueghel was the first out-standing artist who regularly made drawings for the specific purpose of having them copied by others in etching and engraving, himself making but one print. Thus, although by far the most important figure in middle sixteenth-century black and white, he is hardly mentioned in the histories of etching and engraving. His work is the pictorial counterpart of all the legends and popular sayings summed up in the nineteenth century in Charles de Coster's great historical novel, Ulenspiegel. In a period and country predominantly given over to Italianate attitudinizing he struck a note of imaginative realism that in its keenness has never been surpassed.

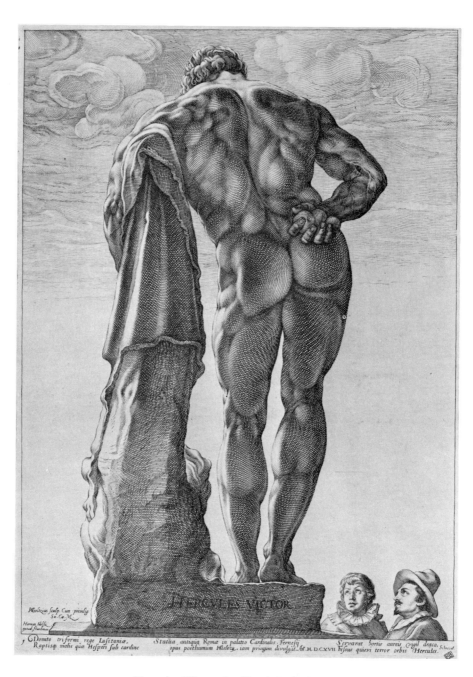

Hercules Victor, by Hendrik Goltzius
$16\frac{3}{8} \times 11\frac{13}{16}$

HERCULES VICTOR

ENGRAVING BY
HENDRIK GOLTZIUS
DUTCH SCHOOL, 1558-1616

Goltzius, taking up engraving where it was left by Dürer and Lucas of Leyden, did more to lay down the lines upon which its future routine development was to proceed than any other one man. One of the greatest technicians and virtuosi of all time, the particular new thing that he introduced into engraving was the swelled line, which is beautifully exemplified in this print of the Farnese Hercules. Its immoderate use is typical of the Northern baroque.

Landscape with a Shepherd, by Hendrik Goltzius

7 ⅛ x 9 ¾

LANDSCAPE WITH A SHEPHERD

WOODCUT BY

HENDRIK GOLTZIUS

DUTCH SCHOOL, 1558-1616

Goltzius's artistry as an engraver fell foul of his own and his time's delight in the virtuosity of technique. As a designer, and probably cutter, of woodcuts, he was on less familiar ground, and in consequence it is in them that his full stature as an artist is most easily seen. Here he struck a chord which in its way has been unsurpassed. His woodcuts were the first outside Italy which were not imitations of pen drawings in another medium.

Saint Catherine, by Rubens
11⅝ x 7¾

SAINT CATHERINE

ETCHING BY
RUBENS

FLEMISH SCHOOL, 1577-1640

 Rubens, the greatest of the Northern baroque painters, made but one etching, of which this is the unique counterproof of the otherwise unknown first trial state. It is specially interesting because Rubens himself made corrections on it in pen and ink, so that it is difficult to say whether it is most an etching or a drawing. In its vigor and generous grace it is perhaps the most important print produced by the Flemish school.

Landscape, by Bolswert, after Rubens

12 ⅜ x 18 ⅞

LANDSCAPE

ENGRAVING AFTER RUBENS
BY BOLSWERT

FLEMISH SCHOOL, ABOUT 1586-1659

 Rubens, following the lead of Brueghel a generation earlier, created about himself a school of reproductive engravers for the purpose of reproducing and publishing his compositions in black and white. These prints after Rubens did more to carry and maintain his fame than his paintings themselves, as they traveled to many places and houses where none of the originals could possibly have gone. The engraved landscapes were of especial importance in the history of the development of landscape, there having been, for practical purposes, no great realistic printed landscapes before their time.

Silenus, by Jegher, after Rubens
17 ⅝ x 13 ⅜

SILENUS

In addition to publishing engravings of his work, Rubens also issued a series of large woodcuts (cut by Christoffel Jegher) which were the last great woodcuts to be made for a period of almost two hundred years. Just as in the case of Dürer, who made engravings, etchings, and woodcuts with his own hand, it is important to notice how much more closely akin the various prints by and after Rubens are to each other than to works by other artists in the same media. Until people begin to think of etchings, engravings, and woodcuts as printed pictures in their times and places, instead of thinking of them in the water-tight compartments of their techniques, it is impossible not only to understand the history of printed pictures but to bring them into relationship to the art, architecture, and thought of their times and places. To study or collect etchings only is like studying and collecting only drawings made with a particular kind of pen. Prints are only printed drawings and except for the technical student it is foolish to differentiate them by their particular techniques.

(95)

Lucas Vorsterman, by Van Dyck
$9\,{}^{17}\!/_{32}$ x $6\,{}^{3}\!/_{16}$

LUCAS VORSTERMAN

ETCHING BY
VAN DYCK

FLEMISH SCHOOL, 1599-1641

 Van Dyck, who was Rubens's pupil, was the greatest portrait painter of his time in the North. While Rembrandt made great portraits, they were originally and are today of far greater importance as aspects of Rembrandt's personality than as likenesses of any particular sitters. Van Dyck's portraits are of importance because they give us dependable professional likenesses of men and women, carried out with great skill and ease, but they have very little emotional value for us on the score of Van Dyck's own personal attitude towards the world. Most of them bear the marks of professional work of the highest rank rather than the marks of artistic creativeness. Of their kind they remain unsurpassed.

The Prodigal Son, by Jacques Callot
7 29/32 x 10 3/8

THE PRODIGAL SON

ETCHING BY
JACQUES CALLOT

FRENCH SCHOOL, 1592-1635

Callot was the first French print maker either to acquire "an international reputation" or to have any influence on the general development of the graphic arts in Europe. Like Claude and Poussin, the two most important French seventeenth-century painters, so much of his best work was done in Italy and outside France that he can be regarded as French only in a rather special sense. One of the great innovators in the technique of etching, he was the first to reduce the operations of stopping out and rebiting to professional practice. He was also the first to effect the intimate *liaison* between engraving and etching which was dominant until the middle of the nineteenth century, especially in reproductive prints. In his clean sprightliness, elegance, wit, and delightful exaggeration of gesture, he may be regarded as the most *spirituel* of the baroque print makers.

Le Bal champêtre, by Jacques Callot

$7\,^{5}\!/_{32}$ x 13

LE BAL CHAMPÊTRE

ETCHING BY
JACQUES CALLOT
FRENCH SCHOOL, 1592-1635

This is one of the most famous of Callot's many landscapes and typical of his etching craft. Prior to his time no one had made such tidy foliage in etching, or had so succeeded in giving depth and rotundity to trees. In this print is admirably exhibited the way in which he was able to produce in etching the brilliance and sharpness usually associated with engraving.

Time, Apollo, and the Seasons, by Claude le Lorrain

$7\frac{1}{4}$ x $9\frac{15}{16}$

TIME, APOLLO, AND THE SEASONS

ETCHING BY
CLAUDE LE LORRAIN
FRENCH SCHOOL, 1600-1682

Claude, most famous of the French artists who worked in Italy, was the greatest of all the landscape painters of the Latin tradition. Where Ruysdael and the Dutch land-scapists portrayed the familiar rustic scene in a spirit of loving realism, Claude, working at Rome and in the Campagna, devoted himself to the creation of ideal landscape, and started an Arcadian tradition that has lasted until our own time. His work is one of the great informative influences in the history of European picture making. An uncertain draughtsman, his etchings have a dreamlike quality that would have been difficult for a more realistic draughtsman to attain.

Anne of Austria, by Jean Morin

11 13/16 x 9 3/4

ANNE OF AUSTRIA

ETCHING BY
JEAN MORIN

FRENCH SCHOOL, ABOUT 1590-1650

During the reigns of Louis XIII and Louis XIV there was a fashion for large engraved portraits, many of which were used as frontispieces not only to ordinary books but to such things as academic theses. The two most important purveyors of these were the contemporaries Morin and Nanteuil, both of whom made prints not only after paintings but after their original drawings. It was the period of Pascal, Descartes, La Rochefoucauld, and Molière, in which wisdom joined hands with wit in smiling sobriety.

Jean Loret, by Robert Nanteuil

$10\frac{1}{4}$ x $7\frac{7}{32}$

JEAN LORET

ENGRAVING BY
ROBERT NANTEUIL
FRENCH SCHOOL, 1623(?)-1678

Where Morin's portraits were etchings, Nanteuil's were engravings. The sparkling, brilliant technique of Nanteuil has somewhat overshadowed the soberer work of Morin in popular favor; but the latter's grasp of character is no less firm, his ability to reach essentials no less remarkable, and it may well be that Morin's plainer statements are far closer to reality.

Christ Healing the Sick, by Rembrandt
$10\,^7/_8$ x $15\,^{17}/_{32}$

CHRIST HEALING THE SICK

("THE HUNDRED GUILDER PRINT")

ETCHING BY REMBRANDT

DUTCH SCHOOL, 1606-1669

 Rembrandt and Callot were the two greatest innovators in the history of etching. Up to their time etching had been little more than a means of printing rather calligraphic drawings. Callot assimilated it to engraving, and by his technical innovations turned it into a codified professionalized technique capable of producing definitely desired effects. The Callot tradition of etching thus became that of the makers of prints after paintings. Rembrandt worked out etching as an exciting and independent art with its own peculiar effects and traditions, among which may be mentioned free (as opposed to schematized) shading, great development of light and shade, the free use of dry point, not only by itself but as an adjunct to pure etching, and the practice of wiping the plate so as to produce tints. His "Hundred Guilder Print" is a sampler of all the various things he was able to do on the copper.

Christ Carried to the Tomb, by Rembrandt
$5\frac{3}{16}$ x $4\frac{5}{16}$

CHRIST CARRIED TO THE TOMB

ETCHING BY
REMBRANDT
DUTCH SCHOOL, 1606-1669

Rembrandt was one of the greatest of all illustrators, having an almost unequaled dramatic sense of the human predicament. In certain ways he is closely akin to Thomas Hardy, who in one of his notebooks finely described the thing that Rembrandt did in plates like this: "The writer's problem is, how to strike the balance between the uncommon and the ordinary so as on the one hand to give interest, on the other to give reality. In working out this problem, human nature must never be made abnormal, which is introducing incredibility. The uncommonness must be in the events, not in the characters; and the writer's art lies in shaping that uncommonness while disguising its unlikelihood, if it be unlikely."

The Three Trees, by Rembrandt

$8\frac{5}{16}$ x 11

THE THREE TREES

REMBRANDT

DUTCH SCHOOL, 1606-1669

Rembrandt's Three Trees is a superb example of the manner in which he was able to orchestrate line into magnificent and atmospheric light and shade, and to produce in black and white the feeling of rich, full color. His paintings of landscape have had little effect upon the point of view or the practice of subsequent generations of artists, but such prints as this have dominated the thought and endeavor not only of later etchers but of many later painters. The great landscape prints by Brueghel bear somewhat the same relation to etchings like this that the music of Bach does to that of Beethoven.

The Vista, by Rembrandt
$4\,{}^{27}\!/_{32}$ x $8\,{}^{5}\!/_{16}$

THE VISTA

DRY POINT BY
REMBRANDT
DUTCH SCHOOL, 1606-1669

Rembrandt was the first to develop dry point into a powerful and colorful medium, especially apt for use in rapid sketching out of doors. In such a print as this, his use of his medium and his method of draughtsmanship have served as the points of departure for a large part of modern work. Such artists as Seymour Haden may be said to have "eaten it alive."

Woman Bathing Her Feet, by Rembrandt
$6\frac{5}{16}$ x $3\frac{1}{16}$

WOMAN BATHING HER FEET

ETCHING BY
REMBRANDT

DUTCH SCHOOL, 1606-1669

 In the last years of his life Rembrandt etched a series of nude subjects, in which he triumphantly showed that etching was better able to cope with the peculiar problems presented by the pictorial representation of the naked body and its atmospheric envelope than any of the then known graphic media. Unfortunately no one since his day has been able to repeat the demonstration.

The Travelers, by Jacob Ruysdael
7 ¼ x 10 ¹¹⁄₁₆

THE TRAVELERS

ETCHING BY
JACOB RUYSDAEL

DUTCH SCHOOL, 1628-1682

 Of all the Dutch landscape painters of the seventeenth century Ruysdael has had the greatest influence on subsequent practice. Many of the English landscape painters just after 1800, especially Constable and the Norwich group, among whom are to be mentioned Cotman and Crome, got so much of their inspiration from him and his fellows that they may truthfully enough be said to have carried on his tradition. From these Englishmen in turn the tradition spread to France where it produced such painters as Rousseau and Daubigny. Ruysdael may thus be regarded as the discoverer of the dominant Northern attitude towards landscape.

La Torre di Malghera, by Canaletto

11 x 16 $^{21}/_{32}$

LA TORRE DI MALGHERA

ETCHING BY

CANALETTO

ITALIAN SCHOOL, 1697-1768

 The soberest of mid-eighteenth-century Venetian painters of views, Canaletto knew how to draw buildings, as no other man before or after, as the media that make sun and air and space visible. His sparkling prints are windows perpetually open upon a smiling landscape that beckons one forth to freedom, the warm sun, and the open sky. From the point of view of technique they are as immaculately clean as a gentleman's linen, and as reticent and unassuming.

One of the Scherzi di fantasia, by Giovanni Battista Tiepolo
8 ¾ x 6²⁹⁄₃₂

ONE OF THE SCHERZI DI FANTASIA

ETCHING BY
GIOVANNI BATTISTA TIEPOLO
ITALIAN SCHOOL, ABOUT 1696-1770

Tiepolo was the last lovely flare-up of the great Renaissance Venetian school of painting, bearing much the same relation to Titian and Tintoretto that the doge of his time did to Dandolo. A Venetian of the mid-eighteenth century with all that that implies, his work is the decorative counterpart of the fantasy and adventure that mark the writings of Goldoni and Casanova. Nothing in it is serious save the perfection of the idle mock-heroic gesture. His technique and work had great influence on Goya, whose life overlapped his, and through him he has taken his place in the so mixed nineteenth-century strain.

One of "The Prisons," by G. B. Piranesi
21⅜ x 16¼

ONE OF "THE PRISONS"

ETCHING BY

G. B. PIRANESI

ITALIAN SCHOOL, 1720-1778

 Beyond question the greatest etcher of architecture that has ever lived, Piranesi represents the romantic aspect of mid-eighteenth-century classical archaeology. More than any other one man he was responsible for the classical fashion in interior decoration that invaded England as "Adam" and France as "Empire." Not only the friend of Winckelmann, but the guide of Adam and the teacher of Clérisseau, he was the great original of whom Hubert Robert was the pale reflection.

L'Embarquement pour Cythère, by Tardieu, after Watteau
19 ⅝ x 28 ¼

L'EMBARQUEMENT POUR CYTHÈRE

ENGRAVING FROM L'ŒUVRE D'ANTOINE WATTEAU . . . GRAVÉ
D'APRÈS SES TABLEAUX & DESSEINS ORIGINAUX . . . PAR LES
SOINS DE M. DE JULLIENNE. PARIS, N.D. [XVIII CENTURY]
BY TARDIEU AFTER WATTEAU

FRENCH SCHOOL, 1684-1721

Immediately after Watteau's death in 1721 his friend Jean de Jullienne started the publication of a series of engraved plates in which he endeavored to reproduce all the paintings and drawings by Watteau. It was the first time any such thing had been tried. He called to his aid the best French engravers of the time, and several of them, especially Tardieu, made undying reputations by the work they did for him. Tardieu's print of L'Embarquement pour Cythère, gay and simple and learned, is justly one of the most famous of all French engravings.

A Bacchanale, by J. H. Fragonard

$5\,9\!/\!32 \times 7\,27\!/\!32$

A BACCHANALE

ETCHING BY
J. H. FRAGONARD
FRENCH SCHOOL, 1732-1806

Fragonard was, artistically, the final segment in the closed circle of French life and thought prior to the French Revolution, effecting for his time and country the synthesis of French academic tradition and the precedents of Venice and Amsterdam. Easy, charming, learned, joining *sensibilité* and gallantry to common sense, he is the final summation of the *dix-huitième siècle*. He gave as much as picture making can of Chamfort's definition of love: l'échange de deux fantaisies. . . .

Illustration by J. M. Moreau le jeune from Rousseau's La Nouvelle Héloïse
$7\frac{3}{16}$ x $5\frac{3}{8}$

ENGRAVING

FROM ROUSSEAU'S LA NOUVELLE HÉLOÏSE
A LONDRES, 1774-1783
BY N. DE LAUNAY AFTER J. M. MOREAU
LE JEUNE

FRENCH SCHOOL, 1741-1814

The eighteenth century produced two very great illustrators of contemporary life and fashion — Hogarth in England, and Moreau le jeune in France. Moreau was not only a most skilled and charming original engraver and etcher, but a professional illustrator, who provided drawings to be reproduced by other men, as may be seen in this plate from Rousseau's La Nouvelle Héloïse. He was the pictorial laureate of French society as it was just before the French Revolution. What anyone makes of the differences between this print and the Hogarth that follows should be of interest to his family.

The Laughing Audience, by William Hogarth
7 ½ x 6 ¾

THE LAUGHING AUDIENCE

ETCHING BY
WILLIAM HOGARTH
ENGLISH SCHOOL, 1697-1764

Hogarth's etching of The Laughing Audience was originally used as the decoration on a printed form for a receipt of money. There having been many thousands of impressions printed from it, it has always been too common to arouse the enthusiasm of collectors, but in spite of that fact it remains one of the most typical and racy specimens of black and white produced in England during the eighteenth century. In its combination of stout, humorous reality and splendid, summary draughtsmanship it is, from the purely artistic point of view, one of the most notable of all English etchings. Hogarth provided the pictorial equivalent of Fielding's prose.

Colonel Tarleton, by J. R. Smith, after Sir Joshua Reynolds
24 ½ x 15 ½

COLONEL TARLETON
MEZZOTINT AFTER SIR JOSHUA REYNOLDS
BY J. R. SMITH

ENGLISH SCHOOL, 1752-1812

 In this portrait of Colonel Tarleton (the celebrated English leader in the American Revolutionary War) after the painting by Reynolds, mezzotinting is seen in its most typical, skillful, bigwigged state. The perfect means for reproducing the classical English family portrait of the eighteenth century, it is the one form of engraving that reached its highest development in England, where it became so popular that it may almost be regarded as a specifically English art. When separated from its contemporary accompaniments in interior decoration the mezzotint loses much of its charm and interest. It is the pictorial counterpart of the furniture of Chippendale and Sheraton.

Mrs. Abington as Thalia, by Bartolozzi, after Richard Cosway

9 ¼ x 7 ¼

MRS. ABINGTON AS THALIA

STIPPLE ENGRAVING AFTER RICHARD COSWAY
BY BARTOLOZZI

ENGLISH SCHOOL, 1727-1815

 The name of Bartolozzi, a Genoese who died as professor at the Academy in Lisbon, is indelibly associated with the peculiarly eighteenth-century British art of stipple engraving. Essentially a reproductive process, stipple took the place of the solider mezzotint for the reproduction of drawings and water colors. It is at home only in rooms filled with the furniture of its time and country, and, like delicious bonbons, soon surfeits.

A psychologist might perhaps draw an inference from the fact that England has excelled in only two graphic media, mezzotinting and stipple, in which line not only plays a subsidiary rôle but is not technically necessary.

Wood engravings from Bewick's History of British Birds
1 ⅞ x 3 ¼ each

WOOD ENGRAVINGS

FROM A HISTORY OF BRITISH BIRDS
NEWCASTLE, 1797-1804
BY BEWICK

BRITISH SCHOOL, 1753-1828

These proofs from the wood blocks designed and engraved for Bewick's History of British Birds, when compared with the Renaissance woodcuts, show as clearly as possible the nature of the innovation made about 1800 in the making of woodcuts. Their combination of technical delicacy and refinement with salty, rough, outdoor subject matter is especially noteworthy. Their point of view and attitude towards life are as typically British of the Napoleonic period as anything that can be found in art or literature. No one has ever better expressed the English feeling for the land and its homely incident.

Illustration by Stothard from Rogers's The Pleasures of Memory
2¼ x 1⅞

WOOD ENGRAVING

LONDON, CADELL & DAVIES, 1810
FROM ROGERS'S THE PLEASURES OF MEMORY
BY CLENNELL AFTER STOTHARD

BRITISH SCHOOL, 1755-1833

Known to students of the history of woodcutting as containing the most sensitive renderings of pen lines on the block made since the publication of Holbein's Dance of Death in 1538, this charming volume is also one of the most interesting of all the many self-conscious experiments in book design that have been made in England. It is the last and most beloved example of genuine eighteenth-century feeling in English typography. T. Stothard, Esq., R.A., who drew its illustrations, was perhaps the most popular illustrator of his time in England, and Mr. L. Clennell, who engraved them in facsimile, was the most gifted of all Bewick's pupils. The titular distinctions copied from Rogers's title-page into the preceding sentence explain a great deal of English art.

The Castle above the Meadows, by J. M. W. Turner
$8\frac{1}{8}$ x $11\frac{7}{16}$

THE CASTLE ABOVE THE MEADOWS

MEZZOTINT BY

J. M. W. TURNER

BRITISH SCHOOL, 1775-1851

Turner, one of the supreme virtuosi among painters, may be regarded as the dead end of the great landscape school that grew up in England at the end of the eighteenth and the beginning of the nineteenth century. Startling and facile, he became the most widely applauded of English nineteenth-century painters, appealing strongly to the upper-class English sentimentality of the post-Napoleonic and Industrial Revolutionary times. Summing up the practice of earlier men, he contributed nothing on which further growth could take place, and opened no doors to future exploration. Like Whistler, seventy-five years after him, he represented the flight from the actuality of life as known in his time. In their virtuosity his mezzotints are the last, pedantic, sentimental phase of the mezzotinter's art.

Spring, by Lucas, after John Constable

6 x 10 1/16

SPRING

MEZZOTINT BY DAVID LUCAS
AFTER JOHN CONSTABLE
BRITISH SCHOOL, 1776-1837

 Constable, gifted with none of Turner's tricky virtuosity, and never pitting himself against the men of the past at their own games, by his innate simplicity and honesty discovered so many things that had not been known before that he became the greatest influence in landscape painting between Rubens and Cézanne. Luck brought to him David Lucas (1802-1881), a mezzotint engraver, and between them they produced the most extraordinary series of landscape prints since Rubens. In them the mezzotint gave its last and its most brilliant flare.

"When the Morning Stars Sang Together," by William Blake
7 5/8 x 5 7/8

"WHEN THE MORNING STARS
SANG TOGETHER"

ENGRAVING BY
WILLIAM BLAKE

BRITISH SCHOOL, 1757-1827

This engraving of the Morning Stars from Blake's Book of Job represents the literary tradition in English picture making at its finest and most lyrical point. It could not have been made at any time or place other than the London of 1825, but also it was not to become popular until the Great War recalled men's minds from the "realism" that came in as justification for the ambitions and the horrors of the Industrial Revolution.

THENOT.

COLINET.

Wood engravings by William Blake from Thornton's The Pastorals of Virgil
Untitled 1 ⅝ x 3 ⅜
Thenot and Colinet 1 ⅜ x 3 ⅜ each

WOOD ENGRAVINGS

FROM THORNTON'S THE PASTORALS OF VIRGIL
LONDON, 1821
BY WILLIAM BLAKE
BRITISH SCHOOL, 1757-1827

This little book is famous for the seventeen small wood engravings that Blake contributed to its illustration. Had one to seek out the most quintessential part of his work it might well be that one would find it among these seemingly so unimportant little woodcuts. A shockingly designed book — from the typographer's point of view one of the world's worst — it is nevertheless by virtue of these cuts one of the outstanding illustrated books of the world.

Thornton, for whom the cuts were made, inserted in his book an apologetic note, saying that Blake "designed and engraved them himself. This is mentioned as they display less of art than genius, and are much admired by some eminent painters." No fuller (or fooler) statement of the essential incompatibility between a certain kind of respectability and art has ever been made.

Illustration by Turner from Rogers's Italy, a Poem
3 ¼ x 3 ¼

ENGRAVING

FROM SAMUEL ROGERS'S ITALY, A POEM
LONDON, 1830
BY PYE AFTER TURNER

BRITISH SCHOOL, 1775-1851

This book marks the culminating point of the development of copper-engraved illustration in England. The most famous of its several illustrators was the great painter Turner, who contributed to it some of his most sparkling and brilliant designs. It has always had a strong appeal to the romantic mind and the myopic eye, and just because it represents in its way the greatest possible care for detail it will probably always hold its fame. A contemporary wit remarked of it, "Were it not for its plates that book would be dished."

Madre infeliz !, by Goya
6 3/32 x 8 2/32

MADRE INFELIZ!

AQUATINT BY
GOYA

SPANISH SCHOOL, 1746-1828

 One of the Disasters of War, done in mixed etching and aquatint, in which Goya recorded his impressions of the Napoleonic invasion of Spain. Since the time of Rembrandt no artist had so drawn the pathos and the misery of life, or come to such rude grips with it. These plates represent the pictorial discovery of the under dog, not in his picturesqueness but in his thinking, emotional agony, and foreshadow the nineteenth century's discovery that the crowd was composed of human beings with immortal souls. It is almost impossible to find even traces of "humanitarianism" in any earlier prints or pictures.

The Diversion of Spain, by Goya
12 x 16 ⅜

THE DIVERSION OF SPAIN

LITHOGRAPH BY

GOYA

SPANISH SCHOOL, 1746-1828

 This is one of the set of four lithographs of Bull Fights made by Goya about 1825. Not only is it one of the first lithographs of artistic merit (the earliest pictorial use of the medium dating from 1802), but it is still one of the finest pictures ever made in lithography. Goya's contribution to picture making may be almost as fully realized in this as in any picture he made. In it can quite definitely be seen the fact that the eighteenth century was over and that a new and wholly different artistic era had begun. It may be regarded as one of the great trumpet calls that ushered in the nineteenth century.

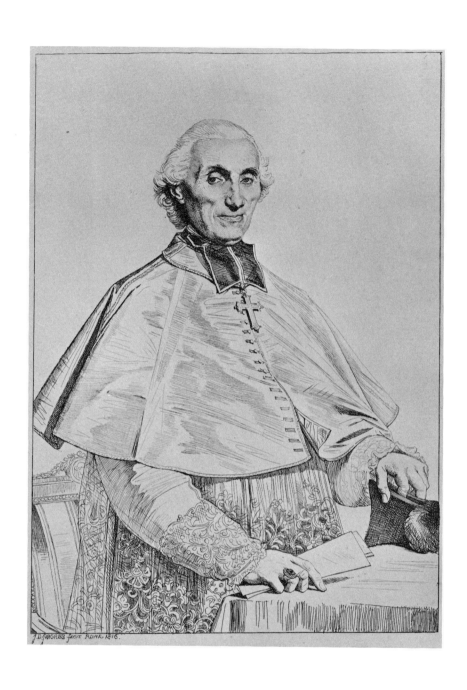

Gabriel Cortois de Pressigny, by Ingres
12¼ x 8⅜

GABRIEL CORTOIS DE PRESSIGNY

ETCHING BY
INGRES

FRENCH SCHOOL, 1780-1867

Ingres's portrait of Pressigny is the only etching he ever made. In its careful, almost pedantic, and rather calligraphic draughtsmanship, it shows clearly how Ingres, one of the greatest of nineteenth-century artists, came out of David and the earlier French tradition of portrait painting. It would be difficult to find anything that bears more strongly the mark of its own time or that is more thoroughly saturated with the academic precepts and the ideals of previous generations. A comparison of the quality of line in this portrait and in the designs for furniture and interior decoration by Percier and Fontaine, the great Napoleonic architects, shows the fact that Ingres was essentially a man of the Empire.

Il grogne et n'ose vous aborder : Il se couche sur le ventre .
il remue la queue . . . .

Lithograph by Delacroix from Goethe's Faust
9 1/32 x 8 1/4

LITHOGRAPH

PARIS, MOTTE, 1828
FROM GOETHE'S FAUST
BY DELACROIX

FRENCH SCHOOL, 1798-1863

The illustrations in this book are original lithographs by Delacroix. They not only brought him his first fame and reputation, but played somewhat the same rôle in the history of French nineteenth-century picture making that Victor Hugo's celebrated preface to Cromwell did to French literature of the same time. It may properly be regarded as the pictorial manifesto of the romantic insurgents of the 1820's. Their spirit is summed up in two quotations from Delacroix's Journal: "Feeling works miracles. By it an engraving, a lithograph, produces on the imagination the effect of painting itself," and "It takes great boldness to dare to be oneself, . . . in fact the boldest of all things is to escape from the accepted and from habits. . . ."

La Juive d'Alger, by Delacroix
8⅛ x 6

LA JUIVE D'ALGER

ETCHING BY
DELACROIX
FRENCH SCHOOL, 1798-1863

Delacroix, the greatest of the nineteenth-century romantic painters, was also one of the greatest etchers and lithographers of his time. This etching of an Algerian Jewess, done in 1833, typifies not only the mad interest taken by European artists at that time in "the East," but the soundness and solidity with which so many of them built up their pictures. It could hardly have been made by anyone who had not undergone the living influence of the great French classical tradition of composition, and shows clearly the reasons why Delacroix in his turn became one of the most influential forces in the development of modern picture making. When its big simplicity is compared with the finicking love of detail that marks so much modern etching, it enables us to understand why Delacroix wrote in his Journal: "Sacrifices. That which it is necessary to sacrifice. Great art which novices don't know; they want to show everything."

Illustration by Johannot from Paul et Virginie
6 5/8 x 5 1/8

WOOD ENGRAVING

FROM PAUL ET VIRGINIE
PARIS, CURMER, 1838
BY WILLIAMS AFTER JOHANNOT

FRENCH SCHOOL, 1803-1852

One of the key books in the history of modern book illustration. The second and the most notable of the lavishly illustrated books issued in France just after the introduction of wood engraving into that country. Meissonier as a young man achieved his first fame as one of its illustrators. Isabey and Tony Johannot were also among those who drew pictures for it. It is the finest specimen of French "romantic" bookmaking. The figures in this illustration were drawn by Johannot, the background by Français, and the whole engraved by Samuel Williams.

LA MUSETTE

O ma tendre musette.
Musette mes amours,
Toi qui chantais Lisette,
Lisette et les beaux jours;
D'une vaine espérance,
Tu m'avais trop flatté:
Chante son inconstance
Et ma fidélité.

Etching by Daubigny from Chants et chansons populaires de la France
$7\frac{1}{2}$ x $4\frac{15}{16}$

ETCHING

FROM CHANTS ET CHANSONS POPULAIRES DE LA FRANCE
PARIS, DELLOYE, 1843
BY DAUBIGNY
FRENCH SCHOOL, 1817-1878

Possibly the last important copperplate book made in France in the eighteenth-century tradition. Among its illustrations are a number of charming etchings by Daubigny, the artist who struck the most authentic Arcadian note of all nineteenth-century etchers.

The Lady of Shalott, by D. G. Rossetti
3 ¾ x 3 ³⁄₁₆

THE LADY OF SHALOTT

WOOD ENGRAVING FROM
"MOXON'S TENNYSON," LONDON, 1857
BY DALZIEL AFTER ROSSETTI

BRITISH SCHOOL, 1828-1882

The illustration of this edition of Tennyson was collaborated in by the members of the Pre-Raphaelite Brotherhood, Rossetti, Hunt, and Millais, and it is not impossible that the future may find in it their best work. Since the "revival" of fine printing in the 1890's (which consisted in great part of the use of much more ink than was necessary) it has become customary to jeer at pale books of this kind, but there can be no doubt that this particular one at least will always be remembered among the greater triumphs of English art. At the present time it is probably at the lowest point of the revolving wheel of taste.

Le Couplet final, by Daumier
$8^{13}/_{16}$ x $6^{1}/_{4}$

LE COUPLET FINAL

WOOD ENGRAVING
FROM LE MONDE ILLUSTRÉ, 1862
BY MAURAND AFTER DAUMIER

FRENCH SCHOOL, 1808-1879

In this woodcut, entitled Le Couplet final and made in 1862, Daumier shows himself creating the type of design which has caused him to be regarded as one of the greatest artists of the nineteenth century, and one of the three or four greatest masters of pictorial composition that France has produced. The influence of such works as this upon painters like Manet and Degas is obvious. It is interesting to notice that, while many painters have been influenced by these Daumiers, with the exception of Forain the primmer and sedater makers of prints have completely failed to learn his lesson. It is probably because in general print makers are primarily technicians and only secondarily artists. It helps to explain why such an overwhelming proportion of the great prints have been made by painters rather than by professional etchers or lithographers.

La Toilette, by Manet
11⁷⁄₃₂ x 8¾

LA TOILETTE

ETCHING BY
MANET
FRENCH SCHOOL, 1832-1883

Manet's La Toilette is merely some woman, no longer a goddess or a heroine from Virgil or Ovid, drying herself after bathing. In it we can see what became of the great classical tradition of subject matter when subjected to the realism, the interest in the here and now, of the third quarter of the nineteenth century. The name, the excuse, the justification have changed, but the great central fact remains the same. From the point of view of technique the print is interesting because it is a kind of etching that could only have been made by a very great painter — never by a professional etcher.

Aux Ambassadeurs: Mlle Bécat, by Degas

$8\frac{3}{16}$ x $7\frac{5}{8}$

AUX AMBASSADEURS: MLLE BÉCAT

LITHOGRAPH BY
DEGAS
FRENCH SCHOOL, 1834-1917

Coming out of the classical tradition of Ingres, and enormously affected by the draughtsmanship of certain Italian primitives, the compositional invention of Utamaro and Daumier, and the studies of light made by Delacroix and Pissarro, Degas found his subject matter through Gavarni and Daumier. It is doubtful whether any other man has ever so combined bitter wit and great learning with acid realism and subtle artistry. His work may be regarded as the pictorial culmination of the mechanistic realism which conditioned most European thought and activity during the late nineteenth century.

La Toilette, by Puvis de Chavannes
12⅛ x 10³⁄₁₆

LA TOILETTE

TRANSFER LITHOGRAPH BY
PUVIS DE CHAVANNES
FRENCH SCHOOL, 1824-1898

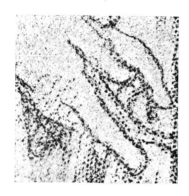

Puvis's La Toilette is thoroughly typical of the draughtsmanship and point of view of the greatest mural painter of modern times. Like Manet's La Toilette it is the kind of print that could only have been made by a great painter and never by a professional maker of prints. The great artist, seeing his medium as a means to an end that lies over and beyond it, is apt to treat it without particular care for its traditional "qualities." The professional print maker by virtue of the fact that he is a professional devotes most of his time and energy to the professional etiquette of his medium—i.e., its traditional "qualities." Very few professional prints are found among the great prints of their times, though in their times they usually have the greatest reputations.

VAN EYCK PINX.   GAILLARD SCULP.

L'HOMME A L'ŒILLET.
(GALERIE DE Mᴿ SUERMONDT.)

L'Homme à l'oeillet, by Gaillard, after Van Eyck
$8^{15}/_{16}$ x $7^{7}/_{16}$

L'HOMME A L'ŒILLET

ENGRAVING FROM LA GAZETTE DES BEAUX-ARTS
AFTER VAN EYCK BY FERDINAND GAILLARD
FRENCH SCHOOL, 1834-1887

Just before the introduction of photogravures the art of the reproductive engraver on copper reached its imitative apogee in the work of Gaillard. No other engraver of paintings has so known how to render the textures of cloth and fur or the minute wrinkles on the back of a bent wrist. This could have happened at no time other than the third quarter of the nineteenth century, when the world was devoting its attention to description of the fact and had yet to learn that the "truths of science" were only explanatory concepts.

Frederick the Great, by Menzel
5⅝ x 4 1/16

FREDERICK THE GREAT

WOOD ENGRAVING FROM SCHERR'S SCHILLER UND
SEINE ZEIT, 1859
BY VOGEL AFTER MENZEL

GERMAN SCHOOL, 1815-1905

Menzel, a young Berlin illustrator, fired by the commercial success of several French books on Napoleon illustrated with facsimile woodcuts, issued in 1840-1842 an illustrated life of Frederick the Great, which was the first lavishly illustrated popular German book published since the Renaissance. An extraordinary and facile draughtsman, he became the outstanding authority on Prussian military uniforms and the pictorial laureate of the House of Hohenzollern. Therefore, after the Franco-Prussian War all loyal Germans regarded him as the greatest of nineteenth-century artists. Within his pedantic limitations no other draughtsman has equaled him. Outside Germany his only influence has been upon certain pen draughtsmen who made illustrations for Punch and other magazines, English and American.

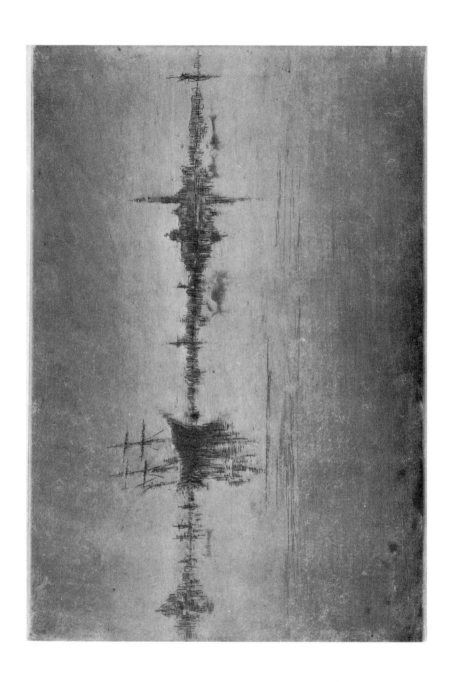

The Salute: Nocturne, by Whistler
8⅛ x 11¾

THE SALUTE: NOCTURNE

ETCHING BY
WHISTLER

AMERICAN SCHOOL, 1834-1903

 Whistler, legally and by ancestry and speech an American, went abroad in his youth, learned his art in France, and never returned to America. He was in consequence always a foreigner, and, having no taproots in either life or tradition, his work was of necessity confined to things that had little relation to either. The exquisiteness of his work is conditioned by its dandiacal aloofness from life. Whether or not life will continue to respect work that denies it, time only can tell. In the meantime, having had the greatest claque known in the history of modern art, he is generally regarded by Americans (though not by Europeans) as "the greatest etcher since Rembrandt."

The Horoscope, by Whistler
18⅛ x 11

THE HOROSCOPE

TRANSFER LITHOGRAPH BY
WHISTLER
AMERICAN SCHOOL, 1834-1903

The work of Albert Moore, Alma Tadema, and Lord Leighton was a sentimental bourgeois attempt to fly from the actualities of late nineteenth-century existence. The fear of life typical of so much English and American work of that time reached its most exquisite and most fragile expression in the work of Whistler. Where the interest in life and the downright affirmations of his great French contemporaries have made them fertilizing influences in modern picture making the world over, Whistler's negative attitude has resulted in the creative sterility of his few followers.

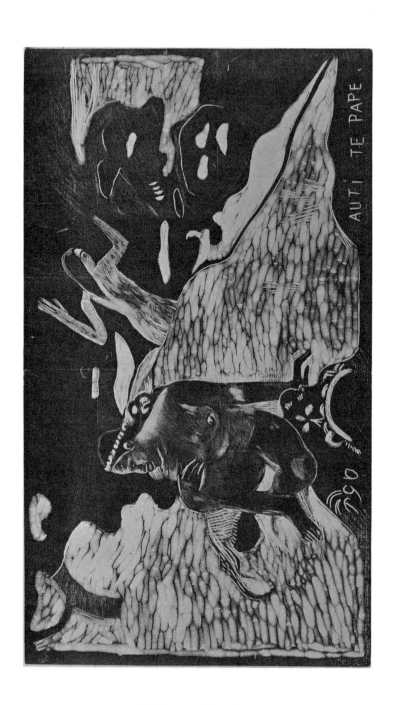

Auti Te Pape, by Paul Gauguin
8⅛ x 14⅛

AUTI TE PAPE

WOODCUT BY
PAUL GAUGUIN

FRENCH SCHOOL, 1848-1903

Gauguin's Auti Te Pape, made in Tahiti by an exile from Europe and its accepted formulae, is a prime example of the new romanticism in its revolt from the excessive attention paid by the factual painters of the last half of the nineteenth century to mere imitation and verisimilitude. Its beautiful pattern and extraordinarily rich color are possible only at the price of giving over too strict imitation of natural forms and textures. Long habit of regarding "accuracy" of drawing as of greater moment than pattern and color prevent many people from seeing in it more than an aberration. But this is like blaming an eggplant because it is not a cucumber.

INDEX

INDEX

Titles of books are printed in italic